Man Poems

2017

A Collection of 100 Poems by Robert McLoughlin

Dedication

To all the dreamers.

Contents

Exit

As she stands up
from her chair
with a pirouette
and swirls her coat off the back
of her chair, seat
then round onto her shoulders,
I know that she is off
to some greater good in her day.

In the Yard

We sat side by side
in rusted, red steel pressed chairs
that rocked when we leaned in them.

She sat with one foot pulled up onto the chair.
With her right elbow propped up onto her knee
and her long slender fingers pointed
upwards towards the tree limbs above us.

As she talked her hand gently turned
and her fingers swayed
with the words which seemed
as if they were travelling along her body
and gliding gently off and out of her exclaiming
fingers.
As the sun glared on this late Thursday afternoon.

Sing Me a Sad Song

Sad songs slow our world.
Memories flood over and over.
Thinking thoughts that
drag along with us
like fishing nets behind a boat,
daily scooping up feelings of
anguish, hurt, and melancholy.
Oh, how some day
we wish that we could just cut
those nets and be free.
to sail the sea with nothing in tow.

Function

I wish I didn't have
to pick up after myself.
It gets in the way of my dreams.

Gourmet

Dinner
Not just meat on a bone anymore.

Boo Boo

So interesting,
how a simple kiss
can still stop all the pain.

Under the Stars

In the quiet night
I can see my sound.
I slip into it
and feel it's crispness,
hear its coolness.
Disguised by the not night light
and announced
by its out of fashion jacket.

At Odds Some Days

Turning the world into squares,
into four-cornered boxes,
with hard right angles
and smooth finite surfaces —
seems to be a predisposition
of humans.

But nature opposes us
with sun circles,
rolling curves,
sensual spirals
and perplexing randomness.
Nice try, humans.

The Music Plays On

Dancing cheek to cheek
would be lovely.
But words took this dance
away from me.
Stepped right in and said to you,
"Excuse me,
but may I have this dance."

The words captured your truth,
as you dropped your hands
from mine.
Turned from me,
and were swept away by innuendo words.
Leaving me standing all alone
in the middle of the dark and gloomy
dance floor.
Shoulders stooped,
head limp on a spiritless body.

Now trying to shuffle off the floor,
as the music plays on.
As other couples dance with their
chosen partners.
As you dance with words
that I neither knew nor invited.
Yet there they were,
and there you went.
Right when we were dancing
cheek to cheek.

Void

I could see how someone
might not want to go outside.
Might want to stay a little longer in bed.
Might skip breakfast,
then have a long lunch
while reading yesterday's paper
full of news of an abstract world.

How a person might sit in a chair
for hours on end,
just gazing out into their yard,
not really watching anything,
not really thinking of anything in particular,
not really feeling anything.

Leaving the dishes for another day.
Not answering the phone,
not checking the mail,
not making the bed.
Sitting down to an open book,
reading just one page,
then having their mind wander off,
not far,
but just away from the page.

Looking around their home,
scanning all their possessions
with empty eyes as if the sculptures, pictures,
books, hats, chairs, and clocks
all belonged to someone else.
How their coffee has gone cold,
their words slipped into canyons of isolation,
and they don't even ask why anymore.
Yes, I could see how that could happen
to someone.

Wishing

So much hope lays
in that small space between
a man and a woman
who are sitting next to each other.

On Top

Ding a ling
Make me a king
Then let me know
Ever so slow
What power is like
What might, makes right

Mystery Woman

She followed me up the building,s steps.
I turned to her and said jokingly,
'Do I owe you money or something?'
She said,
'No, but we could probably work something out.'
I wasn't ready for that.
All I could manage was a smile.
I hope I meet her again someday.

Tea

If the truth be told.
The truth and nothing but the truth.
Truth
Truth
Truce
Tooth
Toot, toot!
Ta, ta!

On and On

She wouldn't stop talking.
I tried to buffer the conversation to an end.
But she just wouldn't stop talking.
So, I was left stranded
on the deserted island of her endless words.

Same Old, Same Old

My life has been normal now
for several weeks.
I don't know how much
longer I can take it.

Birthday

As a boy lay in bed
with the moon overhead
and the shadows of his imagination
twisting thoughts into dream creations…
there slept a young girl
in a faraway place
of fairies, stories and lace.

As he grew older
his dreams grew bolder,
while the young girl began to wonder
if people might be kinder
than what she knew.
So she opened her heart and found it true.

Dreams flowed to fate.
A gift bestowed, an Irish mate.
A glance with their eyes.
Deep silent sighs.
A question
An answer
Then words ever more.
Ever more.

Too Much

Thinking about flowers
in bloom
Then the heat,
the heat that no one suspected
could be so destructive.
No water
No nourishment
Just the heat
bearing down on blossoms.
Smile little flower,
try and bear it just one more day.
Water will shower you with it's
sweet sustenance.
Water will.
Be strong, strong, and wait.
But the flower only knows how to blossom.
Only knows how to smile in the sunlight.
And the heat is confusing.
"Blossom and you will be loved,"
so thought the flower.
The heat.
It's hard.
The heat.
It's hard not to bend,
not to wither,
not to droop,
surely there will be water,
surely.

Always a Thread

Under my desk
which lets me lean and write words,
address letters,
lay down notes of passing importance
and store my objects
for their functional uses,
others for their aesthetic value,
and a few that are kept solely for their sentiment
—
There sit two bundles of white photocopier
paper.
Neatly covered in a thick brown wrapper
with the name of the company
which claims title to the packaging,
the cutting, sorting, and counting of this paper,
which in turn came from a mill
in some rural area where jobs are scarce.
And all the employees punch a time card
and work hard on long, hot summer nights,
amidst swirling mechanical machine noises,
fluorescent lighting, pungent odours,
under indifferent foremen
who tell them
to leave their personal lives at the door.
They are here to work.
That's what they get paid for.

Conversing

You stand and talk
while I sit and listen.
Listen and watch you.
Listen and think of you.
Listen and be consumed by you.
I speak only to hold you.
I speak words to keep you near.
I speak words to lead you closer.
I speak words to let you hear
a faint call from my heart.
I speak to plant thoughts of me
in your being,
awakening long after I leave.

Waking to War

The war is over
Yet I keep my weapon
cocked and loaded.
Not trusting that the enemy
has not just changed uniforms.

Interrogation

Frip
Frop
Cop
Dop
What do you frip, frop?
Would you cop a dop?

Under a Load

He lifts the steel barbells
high above his hearty head.
Shaking and sweating under the strain,
he has proven his prowess.
The weights are dropped with a thud.
With his manly muscles swelled,
he circles the room snorting
like a bull in a ring.
30 stone, a record for him.
People will know him by this:
"Jim Jones, he can lift 30 stone."
He goes home that night
to a lonely wife and a neglected baby.
The wife says there is a letter
from the bank: foreclosure on their home.
She asks him if he had the car repaired yet.
She questions him, again, on things of
importance.
"No!" No to everything, he answers.
His temper flairs,
the baby cries,
she sighs then sulks.
The weight of life is too much for him to bear.
Has been for some time now.
So he goes into the back room,
and lifts.
He lifts the weights that will succumb to him.
He lifts away the weight of the world.
And the more he lifts,
the heavier life seems to grow.

No Deora Mora
(The Big Drops)

The sweet solitary sound
of a lone flute.
With notes that linger
far beyond the
breath or the musician.
Echoing a melody
that draws troubled eyes
to tears.

Statement

I am slouching in my chair here at my desk.
I have been slouching in my chair
off and on since I was six years old.

It feels good, but I know it's not good
for my spine.
But I think why I do it is
more than just because it feels good.
It's an attitude.

I always have felt
a little at odds with authority.
Not enough to throw bricks
or set fire to buildings.
But just enough to slouch
from time to time.

You Seem Disturbed

She said,
Then I said,
Then she said,
Then I said,
Then la, la,
Then la, la,
Then more, more,
Then more, more,

And she said she hadn't said something.
And I said she hadn't the right to say something.
Then the words lost their meaning.
There was only inflection and tone.
Words turned to pure emotion.
Wah, wah.
Hah, hah.

The words got cloudy.
Surrounded us in confusion.
So we paused
until another sharp word
jumped out of our anger
and blew the cloudiness away.
Bare, abrasive words ran headlong
into careless collisions
as we tried to bring
each other to our knees,
with wicked words as weapons.

She said,
I said,
As we sat there with our souls
cut wide open and bleeding to death.
Wah, wah.

Dirty Clothes

Off the hangers and onto my back
in the early morning hours.
Obediently following the twists and turns
of my tossing torso and lingering limbs.
Once only meant for warmth,
now asked to do so much more.
Thousands of threads, coloured, sewn,
pulled tight, cut, trimmed and labelled
by some corporation, from somewhere unknown.
Packaged, flown, trucked, displayed, handled,
held against our bodies, contemplated, admired,
purchased, unpacked, ironed, hung, awaiting
the first day which it will adorn a human body.
Awaiting its chance for fulfilment.
Awaiting the day for which so many have worked
so hard for so little.
For today could be the day
which people look at us.
Today our looks could make the difference.
A new lover finds us, a new boss admires us.
The crowd steps aside for us
as we pass in our new attire.
We are whom we last saw
in the early morning mirror.
We are the knight, the star, the lover, the leader,
who stood in the bathroom light, upright, and
confident, dressed for the role of the day, as the
mirror once again discovers
that we are the fairest of them all.
And if we did it right,
if we made the right purchase,
at the right store,
of the right merchandise,
and placed it on our bodies on just the right day,
for just the right occasion,
we will have all of our dreams

come true and more.
They who know have told us so.
Speaking their wisdom we ever always seek,
their carefully placed proverbs emitting from the
dim blue light of the television
at the other side of the living room.
Yet when day is done, day after day,
year after year,
I come home, strip my body naked to shower the
confusion away,
and in the far corner of my room,
all the possibilities of the day, of my future,
are once again,
reduced simply to…dirty clothes.

A Young Woman

A young woman with a cigarette,
standing with her back to me,
her front to a juke box machine.

One hand on her hip,
the other hand casually flipping
the songs inside the glass juke box.

She turns to one on the list, stops,
head tilting to the side in contemplation.
She is wondering where she was
the first time she heard some song.

She is wondering why he stopped calling her.
Just stopped altogether,
not another word from him.
Not a note, or anything.

She tried calling him,
left messages every day for a week.
Drove to his house, several times.
His friends said he wasn't home.
"Well, please, please tell him I stopped by to see
him."

She wonders now, if she still loves him.
She wonders why she still craves to see him.
After all he did to her, why?
She wonders, and flips to another song in the
juke box.

The Casbah

I wish I knew enough
about foreign lands
to sit at home
in the serenity of my room
making up fantasy
adventure stories
of unfamiliar customs
and high-risk encounters.
But I seldom leave home
and I am unfamiliar with the
ways of the outside world.

Extremes

I think I might do something violent today.
Then I would get arrested, convicted, and
sentenced.
Since I'm a good citizen, the judge would
put me under house arrest.
And I would be able to stay home all day,
just writing, thinking, breathing,
and enjoying the moment.

In the Morning

From a silence,
to a creaking floor above.
Movement,
then tears,
then sobbing from the room above.
Sadness comes suddenly,
knows no clock,
seeks no permissions.

Debt

What you say?
You can't pay.
No way.
What about your boat in the bay?
I might take it away.
If you don't pay.

Two for the Road

harum-scarum
helter-skelter
herky-jerky
hobnob
hocus-pocus
holy moly
hully-gully
loosey-goosey
mumbo-jumbo
namby-pamby
razzamatazz
razzle-dazzle
roly-poly
rub-a-dub-dub
super-duper
walkie-talkie
wham-bam
willy-nilly
wing-ding

In the Beginning

Not knowing from whence I came
Leaves me wondering late into the night.
Wondering if all my days are destined to be the
same.

Wanting life painted neatly in a frame.
Brush strokes soothing my wandering mind.
Not knowing from whence I came.

Looking to give god a name.
Mother, brother, sister, father?
Wondering if all my days are destined to be the
same.

Hoping to one day make chaos tame.
With ordered actions, thoughts and words.
Not knowing from whence I came.

Yet all of this may merely be a game.
If only I could see the humour.
Wondering if all my days are destined to be the
same.

Rising, doing, resting, rising.
'Well done, try again, not good enough,' he said.
Not knowing from whence I came.
Wondering if all my days are destined to be the
same.

Saturday

Simple sounds
soothe souls
Sliding silhouettes
showing sadness.

Green grass
gliding gracefully.
Ghouls gone
gleefully ghosting.

Water waving
wistful wonderings.
White whys
worrying women.

Lonely lilies
lisping lazily.
Longing ladies
lilting lately.

Thinking thoughts
through tears.
Time treads
toughly today.

Fear finds
faceless friends.
Frolicking foes
fume fires.

Hearts hum
holy hymns.
High heads
hear Heaven.

Dear Jimmy,

(Pieces of a torn letter found at the bottom of my empty trash can at the edge of the street in front of my house.)

Hello, how
great. So how
could be better
at Mom's
back
me
goanna
I
be
yah
That's
pretty. It's hard
and Jesse, I'm
have to live
me back? Well
but I don't
I will be
time. I'm
I don't want
back. I don't
bad when you told
me to call. I would
edge. I thought the thing
between me and you? why did
got in a argument? I hate the
here. There's a couple
goanna go on with my
Jesse. I'm so happy for
I wanted to see what Ted
he's going with Amie Jo
likes me. I don't know.
always. Congratulations
Write back soon, please.

Down the Road

Walking in Ireland.
Past crumbling stone walls,
round slender roads
built for commerce by foot.
A brook tingles like
ceramic wind chimes on a breezy night.
Cows could care less.
But the horses lift their big-eyed heads
as I pass by.
Trying to think romantic thoughts
of the ever green country.
Thoughts of simple beauty,
simpler times, and centuries of
clearing field stones.
Nature though, pushes all my thoughts away.
Nature demands my presence.
No room for emigrant songs,
calendar photos, philosophical ponderings.
All in the moment.
All in the walking.
All in the dirt beneath my feet.

One of the Players

I am a very important
person at my workplace.
I even have my own parking space.
It changes daily to random locations
which I must seek out for myself.
They tell me that this
is for my own protection.

We Can Still Be Friends

I wish you a happy…
I hope you always…
May your life forever be…
I am sending best wishes…
I will always love…
If you ever need…
You deserve the…
It was nice knowing you,
and it hurts so much to lose you.

Mistook

He is big,
Baby faced,
violent sized
And he waits his turn.
Looks young.
But I am so surprised
when he talks his rap.
Intense,
with melody,
with meaning,
with depth,
with a love of words.
I want to thank him
as my eyes fill with glistening tears.

Sticks and Stones

It was just a bunch of words.
No knifes or guns,
just words.
Mostly two syllable words at that.
Yet now she hates me more
than the devil himself.

I wasn't paying attention.
Just standing there in the kitchen with her.
Mixing a few thoughts,
a little emotion,
some old memories,
a few projections,
the aroma of new desires,
and some recent observations.

I put them all in the old brain processor,
churned them around a few times,
not particularly paying attention to what I was
doing,
and wham!

An explosion of hard edged, rambling,
thoughtless words
came rushing out straight at her.
Hit her right in the heart
before I even had a chance
to push her out of harm's way.
Assault with a deadly weapon.
I swear, I didn't even know I was loaded.

When Will He Ever Stop?

Turn him on.
The words spill out,
all the words.
Not some,
but all the words
he has built up within himself.
They all spill out,
every last one of them.
In single file
like firemen
sliding down a fire pole.
Rushing words
slipping out freely
because they are not
connected to anything.

Red Hair and Slender Hips

I listened as she talked.
She had a vindictive tone in her words.
I watched as she spoke.
Her forehead was scrunched into angry wrinkles.
I wondered as she vented.
I thought who was it that stole
all the beauty out of this woman.

For What

She told me she used to have a brother.
She said he died in a stupid accident when he was
twenty.
He read about the Marines
and decided to test himself.
He didn't weigh much at all,
but he still put on combat boots, a full back pack.
All the battle gear that a Marine would carry.

Then he tried to swim across a small body of
water
like the real Marines do.
He wanted to be real, too.
With only twelve feet from the other shore to go,
he cramped, sputtered, panicked and drowned.

Now for 15 years,
she has had to tell the story
of a brother who died
because his ego was bigger than his life.
So many others throughout history have done the
same.

Someday

She talked to me about her life.
She was taking even more classes that teach
her how to do things.
Though she said she was not doing anything with
what she learned, at present.
The time wasn't right,
She needed more classes,
more stuff, first.
I wonder if she knows about death.

Perception

She was wrong!
'No, no,' she said.
'Yes, yes,' he said.

Then there was a wall
that he could not climb over,
nor walk through,
nor take apart stone by stone.

A solid wall,
that kept him on the outside
being wrong.
And left her on the inside
being right.

He was wrong?
'Yes, yes,' she said.
'Yes, yes,' he said.

Then she finally
took down the wall
and let him inside again.

Once inside though
he found an empty space.
Or rather
he was empty.

'Yes, yes,' he said.
'Yes, yes.'

Roar

She poked her head in the room.
It was my room
her head.
But it's only my room when
it's just my head.
My, my, my, makes it my room.
So little did she expect
the roar of my wrath
as she just poked her head
in my little room.

In Motion

I've been zigging for some time.
But just now I zagged
and I hope I won't lose my way.

Aging

Life is stretching.
My legs spreading between youth and old age.
Wider and wider…
It is beginning to feel a bit uncomfortable in the crotch.

Chocolate

In a wrapper, so desired,
dreamt of on cloudy afternoons,
longed for when working, working, working.
Patiently set aside while you pay your dues.
Someday…
They told you if you are good,
if you are frugal, if this, if that.
Yet you question, while the sweet smells surround
you.
You wonder.
You think about the rules.
Of who made them and why?
Then you see this thin line of truth.
Slowly you pull on it.
Day after day believing,
until eventually they begin to arrive.
Those sweet things in life.

Family

She said,
'Hi, my name is Denise
and this is Rachel.
I used to date her uncle.

A dynamic I would not have
assumed otherwise.

But once she mentioned it,
I thought to myself
that she did indeed
look like an uncle dater.

From One to Another

Skip a beat.
Beat the heat.
Heat things up.
Up yours.
Yours truly.
Truly you don't think…
Think of your children.
Children of God.
God will punish you.
You are the chosen one.
One day all this will be mine.
Mine eyes have seen the glory.
Glory to the victor.
Victor, a company that makes wooden
mousetraps.
Mousetraps do more than trap.
Trap, it's a trap don't go in.
In your wildest dreams.
Dreams that take us sweetly forward.
Forward into battle.
Battle no more in the fields of daisies.
Daisies, the instruments of 'love me not's'.
Not's and do's,
and don't and wont's,
and words that come and go
with meaning then not,
as the firm fades and the ethereal sails ashore.

In the Eye

I think I'll bring my camera with me everywhere.
People always seem to be at their best
when they think I'm going to shoot them.

Washday

Pushing a grocery cart full of dirty laundry
through the inner-city apartment buildings
and across West 25th street
to the Laundromat.
I am ten years old, my sister is nine.

Mom works long hours,
needs to watch the babies.
Dads a bum,
reason why life is tough.
No clean clothes left, at all, our Mom had
sobbed.

We push our way into this white ghetto
of a Laundromat.
People look up at us, and then away.
Nobody offers to help.
They have no generosity left.

The washers are rusted,
the dryers take dimes and blow cold air.
Soap costs too much, but we didn't know.
We sit and watch the three legged washers
wobble and shake.

The money from the change machine is painted
red.
We don't know why, not even now.
So much we didn't know, luckily.
Cigarette butts on the floor soaking up spilt
soapsuds.
An old woman with no teeth and spurts of hair
stares at us.
It smells hot and musty.
No one talks, or smiles.

The cars on the street outside the Laundromat's
big glass window,
stop and go, stop and go.
And we watch, and watch, and watch.

Then we crunch the clothes warm from the dryers
back into the shopping cart.
Back at home, the clothes in one big pile on the
living room floor.
We sort and fold the now wrinkled clothes,
with our Mom as she sings a Broadway tune from
The Sound of Music.

Empty Pages

It used to be that the words
would not wait.
The images came,
the words for them fell so easily
into the tips of my fingers.
But as of late,
there are few words.
To be certain,
there is no void in life,
only in the symbols for it.
It seems that for now,
I will live my images
without words attached.
Still, it is hard to let go,
hard to grieve their absence
in my life that has always
sought out labels to capture
and parade the act of being human.

Mean Man

The mean little voice
pierced out from the mean little man
who was sitting just across from me.
Proclamations, threats,
and mispronounced words
all shot out
filled with anger
from somewhere deep inside of him.

I felt the vented words stab my body
like dozens of tiny poison darts.
I had to leave the room
to look for the antidote.

God Beams

Waited
Wished
Wanted
for more,
after living on less
for so long.

Glaring

I am sitting here in a coffee house
early on a weekday morning
being watched by a very peculiar man
who I know but often avoid.

He is missing many of his teeth.
Overweight beyond his means,
dresses in homeless piece parts,
and his hygiene leaves me to wonder.

Yet there he sits, three tables away with
his coffee and his eyes on me
as I sit in profile.

He is waiting for my eye contact
so that he can greet me,
accost me with his proclamations.
He is on the hunt,
now and for the rest of the day,
the rest of his days.

Weddings Day

Just after Toesday, comes Weddings day!
Ripe for Wendy's and Tony's who have been
seen sitting in a tree "K-I-S-S-I-N-G!"

And then we grow up...
And what was simple, slips into complexity.
Small worlds widen, histories become attached.
Responsibility feels good, feels rewarding,
feels tiresome, feels a burden and then no feeling
at all.
There are musts, and just becauses.
We wake up and do what comes to us each day.
We lay down at night and hope for that someday
dream.

Then when we least expect it, someone calls
twice.
Someone listens hard, looks long and touches
softly.
And they show up, and keep showing up.
When the other's used to fade,
they stay firm in the thickness of your life.

And the "I" sometimes changes to "we".
And the dream from mine to ours.
And where there was uncertainty, there is now
safety.
And you are still different but now in some ways
the same.
And there is strength in that similarity.
There is love in that sameness.

There are kind words in the darkness of night.

There is a soft shoulder when the world imposes
too much.
There is joy in the exploration of another.
There is a gentle kiss at sunset.
There is peace in knowing you are loved,
when the words are spoken,
"Will you marry me?"

Noble Intentions

Breathing with no intentions.
Like a cat in the green, green grass
on a sunny sun day.
Looking at the uncertain colour
of surrounding, containing, supporting
walls and wondering why, who, when.
Nothing feeling, nothing doing,
nothing changing,
for the minute moment.
Sitting still with no apparent purpose,
no phone calls ringing,
no mail delivering,
no children singing.
Just me breathing,
with these wondering walls.
Should be doing – something?
Isn't there enough of that already?
I can hear the cars zooming by
to fates unknown.
Rains come, go, come again,
to cleanse our human notions
of being all powerful – of all.
While this parrot planet spins.
While the silly solar system spins.
While the unending universe spins.
Some just sit and breathe
with no particular intentions.

The Plan

Nothing is as we expect it
Nothing expects
Expect nothing
Something arrives from nothing
Expect it
Cherish it
As we expect
It is nothing
Yet when we least expect it
It is as we wished
but never expected.

Waiting

To look.
That is all that I ask.
To be looked at.
That is all that I desire.
To have eyes meet,
hearts hope,
and to feel
the fire of passion,
as I stand
in a long line of strangers,
at a fast food burrito restaurant.

Blocking My View

Big hair
on a big girl
is a big mistake.

Home Remodelling

Spending days on end
making things better.
The work required
making things worse.
Continual improvement
being a phrase made
up by some evil capitalistic
multi-tasker.

Just Thinking

I wonder.
I wonder why.
I wonder why and how.
I wonder why, and how, and when, and where.
When I wonder.

More

She sat on my back
to soften the muscles about
my spine,
then cracked my vertebrae.
She could have just
said hello
and that would have
been enough.

Shadow Sounds

The mysterious silence of people
as we go about our daily movements.

The doors held lightly so
they won't slam.
The turned away glances
so that greetings won't be necessary.
The inward thoughts
which will make us invisible,
perhaps even invincible
to all those around us.

Yet, at the other side of the room,
sitting at a table with
cups of simmering coffee
are two women boldly immersed
in a volley of words.
Fuelled by an apparent need
for enthusiastic self-expression
and a need to be heard.
How peculiar.

At a Chinese Restaurant

At the centre of a dinner table
full of women pasted with make-up
and wearing sequined blouses.
With saggy arms, well-worn faces
And voices born from hard lives.
Women who for a few hours
get to be somebody.
They are 'Out on the town'.

Handshake

I shook the hand that
she had offered me.
Then I hugged her
without her invitation,
without her permission.

As I hugged her I felt
I had to say something.
So, I said,
'As long as we're foreigners.'
I didn't know where the hell
that came from.

I'm from Ohio,
She's from New York.
Now, she thinks that
I'm the kind of guy who likes
to press myself up against her breasts
and babbles stuff out of context.

Kick Ass

Get pissed man!
Crank that adrenaline
and go out and do it from the gut!
Make your life big.
Make your every word,
your every movement,
your every hope and desire
so Goddamn important to the world,
that they all step aside
and let you pass right through them
and straight down the path to your destiny.
Go man, go!

Knowing Her

It was the way she crossed her legs,
the way she sighed, almost a moan,
the way the words wisped out of her lips.
Oh, and the way her skin felt when she touched
me.
But now I know she has a heart,
she has a soul,
and she has a hold on me,
which has turned me inside out.

Do You Love Me?

I asked her if she
was in love with me.
She looked right at me
with a long pause.
Then she said, 'No'.
So, I said good,
now that we've got
that out of the way
we can just be friends.
What was I thinking?

When She Stood Up

Hypnotized by her enormous butt,
I wondered what went into its making.

From Use

Worn wood,
I like that.
Worn blue jeans
comfort me.
Frayed edges on the
arms of my favourite chair.
Shoes softened by heat, rain,
and walking.
The yellowing pages of my
favourite book.
The nicks about my big
blue coffee mug.
The grey hairs which speckle
the youth of my hair.

Boys Night Out

Shooting pool,
dark beer,
dark room,
deep thoughts
about the angles
of hard round trajectories.
He leans mean,
smokes a cig,
shrugs off a bad shot.
He used to hold my hand,
sleep in my arms,
listen to my stories.
My little boy has grown.

Who's in Control?

Life like a pinball
in a neon lit pinball machine.
Shot out in the morning
following the straight and narrow path.
Then dropped into a quagmire
of hopeful bonus points,
swinging flippers sending me
every which way.
Temporary lulls
while I will matter
to move at my wanton wishes.
Bells ringing,
lights flashing,
numbers climbing.
But in the middle of all this,
I pause and find myself
falling helplessly straight down the center
between the flapping flippers.
And it is over.
The lights dim,
buzzers no longer sound,
and the numbers are still.
And so am I.

Hoping

I wish I could
I wish I might
I wish I wish
I could I could
I might I might

Road to Ruin

I am eating my own suicide!
Driving.
That's when it happens.

Fast food restaurants
call out to me.

'You deserve this.
Life is difficult and unfair.
Be kind to yourself.
What could it hurt?
Poor baby.'

So, I pull up to the
drive-in window and say,

'I'll have an order of fries,
a chocolate shake,
and a strawberry sunday, please.'

A warrior knife stuck right into the intestines.
Yet, there is no honour in this suicide.

Conversation with a Pissed Person

Yes
Okay
Right
Uh huh
Yep
Okay

Guilt

A frustrated mother.
A priest with a mission.
A worried grandmother.
An angry girlfriend.
Anyone who wants me to go to heaven.
Jesus.
Manipulating politicians.
Marauding Zen Monks.
Lonely people everywhere.
People who have unfair, deep cutting hurts.
Those who must control.
An innocent young child in need.
Those with money and those without money.

In the cold of the winter.
In the depths of grieving our losses.
Whenever we find ourselves too happy.
When we are around prayer.
At Christmas.
At almost any holiday.
When life seems too good to be true.
When we are still.
When we say no.
When we are asked to give.
The Hangman gets out his noose.
The noose of guilt.
And we bow our heads to allow him
to slowly slip it
around our waiting necks.

In the End

Remembering the day
the long hours
the passing minutes
the lingering words
the curious images
the loving touch
the uninvited hurt
the stabbing loneliness
the sound of splashing water
the colour of the chair which
I rest myself upon,
the glasses she wore
the taste of the pastry
the eyes with hidden thoughts behind them
the smell of smoke, still
a long-forgotten photograph
a small unknown trickling tear
a sadness which shows up at the door
when it needs to be fed
and the coolness of the room
which hold the body
that holds the thoughts
which came from a day.

Hatred

She was moving her lips.
Then angry fire spilt out
of them
and onto the table,
flowing onto the floor
towards my chair
and I got my feet up
just in time.

Sustenance

I live a spaghetti life.
All twisted and tied into clumps
of trials and complexities.
Flavoured with spices and red sauces.
Heated with the passion of love.
Simmered with the early morning dawn
of each new day.
I sit down to the table,
pull myself up to my plate,
and slowly make my way,
slurping, twirling, pushing and pulling
at my spaghetti life.

It's a Gas

No romance this week.
Ran out of romance gas.
Kept going on low
for such a long time.
Kept looking for a station
along the way.
Thought I could hold out.
Just cruise on vapours.
Misjudged it all right.
So, now I'm sitting here by the side of the road.
Out of romance and all alone.

Wine and Cheese

She kept telling me stories
about her life.
While her boyfriend kept
inserting his name,
his part in her stories,
in her life.
But she ignored him
and kept telling me
more about her life
without him in it.

Why Yes, I Am

I am uncertain:
When I put my shoes on.
When I take the trash out.
When I drive to work.
When I hold a meeting with people in suits.
When I fall in love.
When I raise children.
When I experience death.
When I take on the trust of others.
When I think about society.
When I think about nature.
When I think about the earth.
When I think about the solar system.
When I think about the universe.
When I think about the cosmos.
When I think about where it all begins, where it
all ends.
I am just not certain.

Sounding Off

The sing song
of her ding dong
as she ping pong
under the wing fong
of the ming ting
loving bing king
by the ling mong
hoping for ring tong
but settling for jing zong
as the soul ging gong.

Ulysses

I helped a quadriplegic friend
get ready to go out tonight.
I put his coat, hat and mittens on him.
His fingers were flopping in different directions,
so I had to hold them together
as I slipped his hands into the gloves.
Sometimes he asks me to drain
the urine catheter bag tied to his leg.
He is a very powerful man,
a solicitor, a member of council,
with weak and withering limbs.
As his body slowly dies,
he becomes stronger and stronger.

After the Ball

'Goodnight, Bob,'
her voice said from across
a darkened parking lot.

She remembered me,
I thought to myself
as I got into my nothing-special car,
and drove away
into the rest of my nothing special life,
feeling loved.

While the Speaker Speaks

From the podium
he speaks of important things,
on and on.
While just behind and beyond him
a man sits at the speakers table.
With arms propping up his head.
One fist on his cheek
the other fist pushing up his mouth.
A light drool ready to appear,
while one eyelid starts to finally droop.

Whoa

Starting down the snowy hill
standing up on my sled
seemed like a good idea,
at first.

Not All Old

It is so unusual to see
an otherwise fully matured adult,
wearing their childhood
on the outside of their being.

For Sure

I knew,
I thought,
I thought I knew.
I thought.
Now new thoughts.
Now I know for sure,
for now.

The Path

Blue eyes,
slow gazes,
wondering glances,
then into her soul I went.

Maybe Someday

I said, 'Do you dance?'
She said, 'Not often.'
So we parted our ways.

There Used to Be...

There was a story.
Which started with an idea.
Which started half way between
my thoughts and my mouth.
'One time, I was...'

And I watched their eyes to see
if they believed.
For if they believed then the truth
was inconsequential
and I was free to tell the story.
To tell a story
just for them.

Go Man, Go

A crumpled man
sitting at a table.
Headphones blasting rock music.
White bandana wraps his scraggly hair.
Jeans all decorated in dirt from where he sleeps.
Head tilted and bent towards the table.
His hands playing on the table.
Drumming the table to the music.
In his mind he is a rock star.
As I pass by his table
I try not to notice.

Enlightenment

A fresh start,
by the sanctifying grace of God,
the girl in the woman is humbled.
Hopeful were her dreams,
under clear skies,
after sleet and the grey sun.

Now so alone,
while everyone,
absolutely everyone
tends to their own needs.
With a pain too deep
to call out.
A destitute heart
that has lost all beauty
and a soul
trampled by reality.

She cried dusty tears,
for love that was not
to be found.
No purpose.
She had none,
and she wandered
in her mind and in the world.

At the edge of it all,
so close to the deep fall,
she raised a hand,
and someone did notice.
Then others saw it too.

No saviours on strong white horses.
Just a few people with smiles,
and a gentle hope.

A thin line to stars
that might shine one day.
So, she pulls lightly on that line,
and each day she is raised up
ever so little.
But she is – rising.
She is rising.

Where I Am From

From my mother
First
Always
From my mother
Light
Breath
Fear
Then the comfort of my
mother's loving breasts.

I am my Mother's son.
I think of that
as anger flares,
values waver,
loneliness overcomes.
I am my Mother's son.

The men
in society's suits,
behind powerful podiums,
with weapons that mangle,
plans that conquer,
egos that crush the weak,
all remain a Mother's son.

At soft sunsets,
melancholy men
melt away
weeping tears inside,
as they are left
behind by all.
A mother's son
left unloved and
so alone.
Through her,
I am.

Through others,
she is.
The caring hand
of another
bears the touch
of my mother.
The deepest eyes
that meet mine –
takes me to the
essence of the woman
who bore me.

Living my life
forever
returns me to
her –
to her life.

Needing her
Leaving her
Losing her
Finding her
In the silence of
nothingness.
In the calamity
of everything
heaped upon my days.
She is there.

From her
For her
By her
I was
I am
I will always be
my Mother's son.

Peace

A word which I saw on Christmas cards.
A dove.
A hand sign from a student with a beard.
Something people fight for?
Something parents long for.

At the edge of a lake, late on a star speckled night.
A lone cricket in the yard.
Holding a sleeping, snuggling young baby.
The moment after you accept death.
Knowing you are truly and deeply loved.

Bing Crosby singing
"I'm Dreaming of a White Christmas".
The Ocean, always, even in a storm, just always.
Sometimes a dog, but it depends on the dog.
Whenever we are quiet with other people, on
purpose and with love.
Every time we climb a tree as high as we can go,
and stay there, with the wind.

When we are able to let go… of things. You
know what things!
The space we always carry with us
but seldom can find.
The thing that we never take but often claim has
been taken by others.
A concept which sells in advertising and
monasteries.
Everyday just a little bit is asked for, please just a
little peace, please.

A political word, religious word, philosophical
word, a radical word, peace!

But words are "not" things.
Words are not peace, not even close.
Peace is the soul, screw the word mongers, the
intellectuals and analyticals.
PEACE MAN -- DIG IT!

Printed in Great Britain
by Amazon